GLADSTONE BAPTIST
1717 English Street
ST. PAUL, MINN. 55109

Children's Prayers for Today

Children's Prayers for Today

AUDREY McKIM
and
DOROTHY E. LOGAN

ASSOCIATION PRESS / New York

Children's Prayers for Today

Copyright © 1971 by Association Press
291 Broadway, New York, N.Y. 10007

All rights reserved. No part of this publication may be reprinted, reproduced, transmitted, stored in a retrieval system, or otherwise utilized, in any form or by any means, electronic or mechanical, including photocopying or recording, now existing or hereinafter invented, without the prior written permission of the publisher.

Many of the prayers were published originally in the United Church of Canada's publications: *Wonder, World Friends,* and *Surprise.*

International Standard Book Number 0-8096-1833-8

Library of Congress Catalog Card Number 78-167881

PRINTED IN THE UNITED STATES OF AMERICA

The Prayers

MORNING AND EVENING

page   8   Time to Get Up
9   When I Can't Go to Sleep
10   A New Day
11   Just a Minute
12   Tomorrow We Move Away

GOD AND MY SELF

14   My Secret Place
15   Who Are You, God?
16   I Am I
17   Inside Me
18   Questions
19   Keep My Temper
20   Forgiving

WITH MY FAMILY

22   My Dad
23   Living in a Family
24   My Sister's Too Pretty
25   Even Though I'm Sick in Bed
26   No One's Home
27   Help Me!
28   After Someone Dies

SPECIAL DAYS

30   Vacation
31   Grace at a Picnic
32   It's Today!
33   Thanksgiving Time
34   Christmas

AT SCHOOL AND PLAY

page 36 My Problem
37 Bullying
38 I Can't Find a Friend
39 When the Teacher Scolds
40 Help My Friend
41 That Awful Boy
42 I Have a Friend, God

GLAD AND SAD

44 God, You Did It All!
45 Kittens
46 A Lie
47 Rain on Me
48 Pain
49 New Glasses
50 Homework

PEOPLE EVERYWHERE

52 Faces of Hate
53 Children in War
54 There Was an Accident
55 City Street Kids
56 For a Newcomer

WONDERFUL WORLD AND THINGS

58 Thanks for My Eyes
59 Beside the Ocean
60 Colors
61 Better Than Television
62 Dandelions
63 Your Sand and Stars
64 Wonder-Full

MORNING and EVENING

Time to Get Up

It's time to get up, God,
and I'm lying in bed.
My eyelids shut out everything
but my thinking.
What if I open my eyes
and there is nothing?
What if I look outside
and there is nothing?

Such ideas of nothing make my heart pound
and my blood rushes around
in my body. I can't keep my eyes shut.
I open them and everything I see looks fine.
Even the crack in the plaster makes me grin.

I jump up and look out of my window.
Your world is there, God; sky and trees.
Our world of balcony windows, TV aerials,
haze, and one pigeon soaring.
Good morning, world!
Good morning, God!

When I Can't Go to Sleep

When I'm afraid,
I like to think that you are near, God.
Help me to feel sure of you,
and not be afraid.

When I see strange things in the dark,
help me to remember that my eyes get tired
and play tricks on me.
Help me let my eyes rest, too.

I know you are with me,
and that is good to know.
I know everything will be all right.
I know you, God.
I know . . .
know . . .

A New Day

What will this day be like?
Sunny? Rainy? Hot? Cold? Exciting?
Mom has just called me to get up for breakfast.
And this whole day is still a surprise.

What will happen to me?
What things will I do?
A good laugh with Mom?
A ride home with Dad?
A secret hour all to myself?
All these surprises
from you, God, to me, with love.

And for you, God,
some special thoughts,
some plans,
some play, some work.
Some real feelings
from me to you, with love.

Just a Minute

Hey, God—
Just wait a minute.
Let's stand still.

I don't have anything
to talk to you about.
I just need to think.

There, that's better.
Thank you, God.

Tomorrow We Move Away

Tomorrow, God, I won't be sleeping in this house.

I'll be talking to you, next time,
in my new house far away.
You'll be there, too, won't you?
Make the new house seem like home, God,
because this one has been so much fun.

Perhaps another boy or girl will sleep in this house.
Make them happy too.
They won't know about me,
but I hope they'll love this house,
and get to know all my old friends here.
I think they'll find out you love them, too,
because this is a good house.

GOD AND MY SELF

My Secret Place

I call my secret place a cave!
No one comes in but me.
No one else even knows about it.
I hide there when I need a quiet spot.
It's dark, and safe, and kind of warm.

Thinking is what I do in my cave, mostly.

If anyone else really understood about this place,
and really liked me,
and wouldn't laugh and tell about it, later,
I'd invite him in.
But I haven't found that person yet.

God, you are in my secret place,
but no one else, so far.
It's my very own!

Who Are You, God?

I wish I knew
who you are.
I'd like to be sure.
They say you love me,
they say you help me,
but I don't know just how.

Wondering about you,
I think of people who love me,
and that helps me know you a little.
I talk to you inside myself,
yet you're bigger than the whole world.

Help me, God,
to find out who you are.

I Am I

I am I.
But no one seems to care about that
but me—
and you, God?

I am I.
I feel.
I decide.
I create.

But I don't like how I feel today.
I can't make up my mind what to do.
I just lie around doing nothing.

Well, I *am* thinking about me,
and about you, God.
If we work together,
how will I feel?
what will I decide?
what will I do
that no one else has ever done before?

I am I. You are God.
So anything might happen!

Inside Me

Inside me must be a strange place.
All the things I do
and all the ways I feel
and all the ways I act
start inside me.

There are my bones and teeth
to start with.
Then there's the food I put inside.
But I—the inside "I"—
am more important than these.

I have feelings, like happy and cross.
When I remember my birthday or Christmas,
all the sounds and pictures and smells
come back inside me somewhere.
Things I've forgotten must be in there.
Are they lost, or will I find them again?

Learning how to skate
and kissing Mom and laughing at jokes,
all these start with this inside "I".
Crying and feeling and working hard, too.

Maybe that's where you are, God.

Questions

Is praying to you
talking to you, God
and then listening
to what you say?
Is that what praying is, God?
Do you speak to me
through my mind?
Or is prayer something more?
Help me to know, God.
I have so many things to pray about.

Keep My Temper

Today will be better
if I can remember you, God.
Please help me keep my temper.
O God, I do want to be calm.
Help me to think first, then speak slowly,
without blowing up, and then being ashamed.

I'll think of you cooling me down,
I'll think of you reminding me not to shout.

Please give me some more strength.
I need it to make me smile instead of yelling.
You'll see a difference, God.

Forgiving

It's a funny thing, God.
I just found out
about forgiving.

I knew about forgiving,
I guess—
but I didn't know how, really.
I just said the words,
and felt cheated, somehow.

Now I just did it—really did it—
for the first time.
Norman told the teacher I was hiding something.
I was going to get him at recess.
But I looked at him
and then, for some reason or other,
I felt different.
Something inside me
didn't need to get even.

I felt all right.
I even smiled.
God, you know what I mean.

WITH MY FAMILY

My Dad

You know my dad, God?
He's a great guy, isn't he?
But he works too hard every day.
He's really uptight when he gets home.
Then we try to get him to relax.

But sometimes we make it worse for him
by our quarreling and noise
and using the phone all the time.
We don't want to be like that.
We like to hear him laugh
and have him fool around with us.

Help us all to give him lots of fun
whenever he needs it,
even when fun to him means peace and quiet!

Living in a Family

Our family is noisy.
We all want to be heard.
We don't like listening.
So I give up
and let the voices roar around me.

God, help them to listen to what I say.
Help them to understand.

They say I don't listen, either.
I thought I did.
Help *me*, God, to listen to *everyone*
in my family.
So we can all learn to live with each other better.

My Sister's Too Pretty

My sister is too pretty.
She's got everything!
And I'm skinny and a nothing
when I think about my eyes, and hair and my *nose!*
Oh, I hate my looks!
It wouldn't be so bad if *she* wasn't so pretty.
Everybody says lovely things about her.
Then they look at me
and they stop and try to think up
something to say that's nice.

I want to like my sister.
Sometimes I do when we are alone together.
Sometimes I even feel proud she is in our family,
but not very often!

Help me, God, not to think so much
about *her* looks when I think of mine.
Help me to think that looks aren't all that important.
That's the hardest to do!

Even Though I'm Sick in Bed

Thank you, God,
for all the people who do things for me
while I'm sick in bed.

Thank you for Jo-Ann, who gave me one of her kittens.
Thank you for Sam, who fixed my pencil box three times.
Thank you for Aunt Sherri, who let me use her bed table.

Thank you for Mom, who has to nurse me now.
Thank you for Dad, who goes to the library for me.
Thank you for George and his puzzles.
Thank you for Beverley and her card games.

What do I have that I could share with them?

I have love—lots of it!
You share love with me, God—
I can give it back to others.

No One's Home

God, walk up the steps with me.
God, stand near the door with me.
God, put the key in the lock with me.
God, turn the knob with me.
God, walk right in with me.

Empty house, here's God and me to fill you up!
Empty rooms, here's God and me to make some noise!
Together, we'll put some life in this house
until the others come home.

Then God, please stay with us all.
It's good to feel you're at home here with us.
Thank you, God.

Help Me!

I'm up here in bed.
They are yelling at each other downstairs.
I put my hands over my ears.
But after a while I hope they've stopped
and I listen again.

They are still yelling!

O God, help me not to hate them
when they shout at each other this way.
I think they like each other sometimes;
this morning we were all laughing.
I love them. Honest, I really do—

But please help me not to hate them now.
Help me! Help me!

After Someone Dies

I didn't think I'd ever feel like this again,
but it was great today, God.
Thank you for all the fun I had.
I walked to school with Barry,
you know, my new friend—
and we laughed all the way.

Last evening all our family were at home,
and Dad played Ping-Pong with Beth and me.
My grandad used to do that, but he died
on Tuesday.
Mom had to go away to the funeral.

But now she is back, and we all talked
about Grandad,
and we feel happy again.
Thank you, God, for helping us know
that you are with Grandad and with us too.

Special Days

Vacation

Thank you for vacation time.

When you thought up summer,
did you know it would be just right
for vacation?
I think it's great.
It gives me time to do the things
I've thought up during the year.

My cousin Ronnie in the country wants to visit me.
And I want to get away from the city where it's hot,
and visit him.
If we do it will be great.
If we don't, well, maybe there will be
other things to do.

Vacation time is beautiful.
I'm glad it's here.
Thank you, God, for all these holidays
ahead.

Grace at a Picnic

Can't stop now, God!
Thanks!
It's really terrific!

It's Today!

It's here! It's here!
Today has finally come!
The day I told you about, God,
filled full of fun
and good times, and people dancing.
I feel like firecrackers inside me.
Dance with me, God!
Dance with me, everybody!
Jump for joy with me.
Wave banners,
and beat drums,
and blow horns!
Everything is wonderful today.
Everything makes me so happy!

Thanksgiving Time

At church on Thanksgiving,
when they pile up all those fruits and vegetables,
it stands for all the things we are thankful for
and how we ought to think about sharing.
We have so much and others have so little.

My favorite food is the kind I eat
without using forks or spoons.
You know, hot dogs, chips and cones,
and things like that.
But it tastes best when I share it.
I wish I could share it with all the kids
in the world who need food.

I'm glad Halloween is close to Thanksgiving.
I have fun collecting loot,
but I'm glad it gives me the chance
to collect for UNICEF, too.
When my UNICEF box bulges
I know hungry children in other parts of the world
who need milk and other good food will get some.

There must be other things we could do
to share the good things in your world, God.
Help us to find more ways that we can share.

Christmas

Thank you, God, for making today come true.

Thank you for all our hoping and wishing.
        It took a long time to come,
        but it's better than ever.

Thank you for all the working and buying and cooking.
        We tried hard to make each other happy,
        and we have.

Thank you for all the singing and laughing and eating.
        We are finding out about happiness,
        we are living in joy.

Thank you for all the other gifts that we can't see.
        We think you must have other secret surprises;
        gifts that can't be seen or heard or touched.

Thank you for Jesus, our Brother, today and always.
        We are giving a family gift to him
        on his birthday—
        all our love.

At School and Play

My Problem

            God, I have to tell you about this week.
Monday: "Look at the brand-new bike!"
            They all crowd around
            and touch it, yelling and admiring.
            "It's really mine!"
Tuesday: They all want to try it out,
            but I'm saving it.
            No one can ride it but me.
            I'm the owner!
Wednesday: For two whole days
            this is the way I act.
            Slowly, word gets around.
            They all believe me,
            and go home to their old bikes.
Thursday: Now I sit on the porch
            and think hard and long.
            Being the owner isn't that much fun.
            Why don't I enjoy that bike more?
Friday: "Hey, Fran and Mike!
            See if my new bike fits you!"
Saturday: "Hey, Don and Cindy!
            Come on for a ride!
            I'll ride yours, and you can ride mine!"
Today: So you see, God, what happened—
            I've learned something about being an owner.
            Thank you for this week, God.

Bullying

All the guys are picking on Archie again.
He's so easy to tease,
and push around.

I laughed at him, too, today,
and I felt mean.
I can't help thinking
what it would be like to be pushed around that way.

Help me, God, to do something
like standing up for old Archie.
It scares me just to think about it.

I Can't Find a Friend

I'm all alone, God.
No one will play with me.
There's only the mirror to talk to.

I can see my frowning face.
I can hear my whining voice.
I can feel my aching throat.
This isn't much fun.

I need you here, God.
Please help me.
Well, I'm not really alone, am I?
You're here.

If I were those kids outside
I guess I'd want to play with someone friendly.
God, smile through my face,
laugh in my voice,
share with my hands,
and help me to look for someone
who wants me as a friend.
I'd be glad to find someone like that.

When the Teacher Scolds

God, come closer!
I feel so little—and so hurt.
The teacher didn't listen to me.
But I said things all wrong, anyway.
God, keep me from crying.
Make me strong, so I can work better.

Help me sort out my words faster next time,
so the teacher won't think I'm sulking.
Please help her to understand what I'm saying.
I didn't mean to do anything wrong.
Help her to find that out, somehow.

We both spoiled this morning.
Give us a fresh start this afternoon.

Help My Friend

God, you often help me,
so please help my friend who needs you.
She doesn't know much about you,
so I'm asking for her.
She really needs it!

She's crying—I can't get to her.
She doesn't know you help people.
She thinks she's all alone.

There's something you can do, isn't there?
Maybe I can tell her
that you're her friend.
God, be close to her.

That Awful Boy

If I pray for him, God,
will he stop being mean to me?
Can you love him
when he's so awful?
I guess you can—but I can't!
Can you help me like him?
Could you even help him like me?
I sure hope so.

You love me—and I'm pretty awful sometimes.
If you could only show me
something good in him, to start with.
Maybe he's better when I don't see him.

Be the friend of both of us, God,
and that will give us something to start on.
Help us get ready to be friends.

I Have a Friend, God

One of my best friends—
the one called Nikki—
is so pretty and such fun.
My mother says, "She's such a lovely girl!"
Well, Nikki dared us to pinch a lipstick
from the drugstore today.
Terry took her dare.
I was scared and didn't.
But I didn't say anything, either.

Anyway, God, Nikki is my friend
and I love her.
She's going to want to pinch things again.
I know she is!
What do I do now, God?
Help me.

GLAD

and Sad

God, You Did It All!

O God, I'm singing for joy!
Listen to me—I'm full of music!
Your world is so full of nice things,
I can never see and taste and feel them all!

Thank you for thick, warm blankets.
And thank you for chocolate ice cream.
Thank you for new books to read,
and for my dog's wagging tail.

God, you did it all!
You gave me all this joy!
I shout, and run, and slide down hills,
and roll over and over, just for happiness!

O God, you make me so happy!

Kittens

I know you made puppies, God,
and even ponies and rabbits,
but I think your very best thing
is kittens.

Kittens are so soft and bouncy,
and their mouths smile when they mew.
They purr all the way through their stomachs,
and lick my face and bite my nose.
They always have such a good time.

I'm glad you made kittens.
They make me feel happy.
I just can't tell you, God, what it is
That's so wonderful about kittens.
But you know, don't you?
You must feel that way, too.

A Lie

I told a lie.
I was so scared they wouldn't like me
if they knew what I did.

But I don't like myself now.
They think Robert is to blame,
because I told a lie.

Please, God, help me tell them
that I told a lie.
I want to like myself again.

Rain on Me

When the rain is dripping, dropping,
Over house and factory,
Lifting up my face in welcome,
I am glad it rains on me.
                Rain is pouring, rain is free,
                Shining rain from God to me!

On the bricks and eaves and shingles,
On the bird and ant and bee,
On the trucks and buses falling,
I am glad it rains on me.
                Rain is pouring, rain is free,
                Shining rain from God to me!

Thank you, God, for all the showers,
For the drops that splash on me;
In your world of clouds and rainbows
I am glad it rains on me.
                Rain is pouring, rain is free,
                Shining rain from God to me!

Pain

I can't get away from this pain.
I hurt all over!
Everything else seems far away,
and all I can think about
is how much it hurts.

God, why does it have to hurt?
Can't you stop it?

You *do* know how bad it is, don't you?
I feel you sharing this pain with me.
You're helping me hold up this load of hurting.
The pain is still here, but you're here, too.
And that helps.
God—I need you near me.

New Glasses

God, look at me now.
Don't I look different?
I have these new glasses to wear
everywhere I go, even out playing.
Do you think they look funny?
Some kids laughed this morning,
and for a while I wanted to take them off.
God, help me to get used to them,
and not think about how I look.

Wow! When I think about the street
I want to go right out and look again!
It was just like a picture—
people in cars,
and signs all bright and clear,
and even stones and leaves and cracks.
I could see everything!

I'll bet you had something to do with doctors,
and testing, and glasses, God.
Now my eyes are better than before,
and I can see what everything's really like,
just the way you intended me to!

Homework

I've been having trouble with homework, God.
Before I open my book
I want to ask you something.
Will you help me?
I'm afraid I'll get stuck before I'm done.
You know how hard this stuff is, don't you?
When I'm halfway through,
will you give me, please,
an extra push
so I'll make it through
right to the end?

PEOPLE EVERYWHERE

Faces of Hate

I saw fighting on TV tonight—
Faces full of hate,
yelling, screaming.
Why do they do that, God?
People look so ugly when they hate.

Help us all, dear God
to give this world
more faces full of love
than hate.

Children in War

God, I see and hear about children
crying in faraway countries
where there's war, and fighting and death.
It's not fair!
Why do they have to hurt and kill little children?

When they're hurt, these faraway children,
give them healing sleep,
and kind doctors to help them.
When they're afraid, give them courage,
and friends, and shelter from the bombs.
When they're lost, or left alone,
give them hope,
and a strong hand to lead them to safety.

God, I don't know how to help all by myself.
Show all of us how to help together.
Help these children to find out
that you are their loving Father
and that no trouble can stop you from helping them.
Help them to know that someone cares.

Help us all to bring peace
and quiet homes for them again.

There Was an Accident

I saw the cars lying smashed and twisted.
I saw the police, and the flashing ambulance lights.
I saw all the people standing around,
and glass and oil and skid marks on the highway.

I feel sick and afraid.
Are they hurt and bleeding—or dead?
I'm crying because it's so awful to see.
I can still see it, even though the policeman waved us on past.

God, be in someone's arms, ready to hold.
Be in someone's voice, kind and strong.
Be in someone's helping hands.

I'm afraid for myself, too.
It could have been our car.
Let me feel you're near me, God.

City Street Kids

We went for a drive this evening, God.
We took our aunt from Europe to see the city.
We were proud to show her our parks,
our new buildings, our best streets.
And then we went into the old part of the city.
So many people! They slowed us right down.
They seemed to be too many for each street.
My parents were upset about it.
And said it was a shame the way some people have to live.
And I know our church is helping build a big housing project.

But you know, God—
The kids were having a great time.
They were all out playing games—
dozens of them, everywhere!
I wish I had that kind of fun.
We don't play like that on our street;
the lawns are off limits—
no room at the back—
we use our rec room or the plaza.

Do those kids wish they were us?
There should be a better mix, shouldn't there, God?
Help us to find out how to do it, please.
I liked the look of those kids.

For a Newcomer

God, you know the words Angelo knows.
He's afraid, and new in this country,
and he can't talk to us yet.
You can talk to him, though.

How can I be kind to him
without words?

I know—I can smile, can't I?
I can stand beside him at recess,
and throw the ball to him.
And I can tell him my name!

I guess you got me started, God.
Thanks for your help.

Wonderful World and Things

Thanks for My Eyes

I've been learning about eyes today.
Each eye is like a super camera.
It has a lens and a shutter.
The film develops at once.
Camera inventors used eyes as models.

How did you ever think up eyes, God?
Mine, and all the millions in the world?
I keep blinking when I think about it.
Eyes! Eyes! Wonderful eyes!

Beside the Ocean

How much ocean there is!
I knew you made it all, God,
but I never thought it would be so big!

It's calm and shining now, and bright, bright blue.
The waves ripple in and out.
But I've seen the wind make loud breakers,
white foamy waves, riding in on crashing surf,
shaking the earth with their thunder.
It made me shake, too, God.

It's all your ocean—thousands of miles!
All your sand—millions of grains!
All your fish—and crabs and whales, and oysters!

This ocean is too big for me.
But I like thinking about your bigness, God.

Colors

The more I think about the colors
I see, God,
and how many beautiful ones there are,
the more I think how wonderful that you
thought them up.

And then, all the things you made
in colors,
Wow!
I keep thinking and thinking—
I want to use colors, God,
to make beautiful things too.

Thank you, God, for a world of color.

Better Than Television

Which is greater, God
TV or my mind?
TV gives us all kinds of shows and movies
and things.
But my mind can make up all sorts of things, too.
TV is one of the greatest inventions.
But we need eyes, ears and
a mind to make sense out of TV,
or it wouldn't be worth a nickel, would it?
Eyes, ears and minds are *your* inventions, God.
Nobody can beat them!
Which is greater? TV or my mind?
I don't have to ask.
I'll take my mind any day.

Thanks for inventing my mind, God.

Dandelions

I'm upside down on the grass,
and my eyes are looking up
at dandelions.

What a wonderful surprise!
Millions of baby suns in our grass—
and I had to stand on my head
to get my first good look
at dandelions.

God, thank you—and yippee!
Everywhere I go now
I see these yellow stars
waiting for me to lie down
and see millions and millions
of sunny faces laughing!

Your Sand and Stars

Some say the world just happened.
Others say that you made it, God!
You were the inventor.

I visit an observatory
and see that bits of sand
make glass.
Glass makes a telescope.
A telescope sits in our observatory.
I see one star through it—one—two—three;
A great galaxy of stars
millions of miles away.

Behind the bit of glass
a human mind to make a telescope.
Behind the human mind, the tiny bit of sand,
and the galaxies—
You, God. That's what *I* think!

Wonder-Full

I wonder at millions of tiny grass blades.
I wonder at waves that keep curling ashore.
I wonder at cats,
    and at moles,
        and at whales.
I wonder at sand,
    and at thunder,
        and fire.
Seeds into flowers!
Ice into water!
Night into day!
Young into old!

God, your world is full of wonders,
And I am wonder-full—just *full* of it!

GLADSTONE BAPTIST CHURCH
1717 English Street
ST. PAUL, MINN. 55109

11-15